God's Little Instructions for Women

D0445884

P.O. Box 55388
Tulsa, OK 74155

God's Little Instruction Book for Women
ISBN 1-56292-222-X
Copyright © 1996 by Honor Books, Inc.
P.O. Box 55388
Tulsa, Oklahoma 74155

3rd Printing
Over 197,000 in Print

Manuscript prepared by W.B. Freeman Concepts, Tulsa, Oklahoma.

God's Little Instruction Book
for Women

Introduction

God's Little Instruction Book for Women is a collection of dynamic quotes and sayings spanning the wisdom of the centuries. Each quote is accompanied by a parallel portion of Scripture, with an emphasis on the practical and spiritual experiences of today's women. Together they offer comfort and guidance, hope and encouragement—and even a good laugh or two.

This little book was designed to be fun reading, yet thought-provoking. It will challenge you to expand your outlook and to fulfill your potential as a woman. Whether you are active in a business or in the home, these timeless thoughts will recharge your inner being and give you sound advice as a bonus. Enjoy your time absorbing these pages—many of them were written just for you!

And they that know thy name will put their trust in thee: for thou, Lord, hast not forsaken them that seek thee.

Psalm 9:10

*M*y job is to take care of the possible and trust God with the impossible.

When Mother Teresa received her Nobel Prize, she was asked, "What can we do to promote world peace?" She replied, "Go home and love your family."

Let love and faithfulness never leave you; bind them around your neck, write them on the tablet of your heart.
Proverbs 3:3
NIV

Humble yourselves in the sight of the Lord, and he shall lift you up.

James 4:10

You are never so high as when you are on your knees.

*G*ive your troubles to God: He will be up all night anyway.

He will not allow your foot to slip; He who keeps you will not slumber.

Psalm 121:3

NASB

A man hath joy by the answer of his mouth: and a word spoken in due season, how good is it.
Proverbs 15:23

We should seize every opportunity to give encouragment. Encouragement is oxygen to the soul.

You may give without loving, but you cannot love without giving.

For God so loved the world, that he gave his only begotten Son, that whosoever believeth in him should not perish, but have everlasting life.
John 3:16

...for he hath said, I will never leave thee, nor forsake thee. Hebrews 13:5

When I come to the end of my rope, God is there to take over.

14

*T*he Lord can do great things through those who don't care who gets the credit.

A man's pride shall bring him low: but honour shall uphold the humble in spirit.
Proverbs 29:23

A happy heart makes the face cheerful.
Proverbs 15:13
NIV

*W*hat sunshine is to flowers, smiles are to humanity. They are but trifles, to be sure but, scattered along life's pathway, the good they do is inconceivable.

I regret often that I have spoken; never that I have been silent.

In the multitude of words there wanteth not sin: but he that refraineth his lips is wise.

Proverbs 10:19

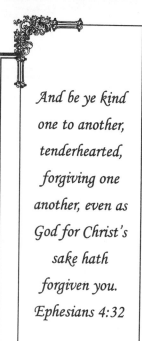

And be ye kind one to another, tenderhearted, forgiving one another, even as God for Christ's sake hath forgiven you.
Ephesians 4:32

"*I* can forgive, but I cannot forget," is only another way of saying, "I will not forgive." Forgiveness ought to be like a canceled note—torn in two, and burned up, so that it never can be shown against one.

Worry is like a rocking chair: It gives you something to do, but doesn't get you anywhere.

Casting the whole of your care—all your anxieties, all your worries, all your concerns, once and for all—on Him; for He cares for you affectionately, and cares about you watchfully.

1 Peter 5:7

AMP

*In my distress I
cried unto the
Lord, and he
heard me.
Psalm 120:1*

*L*ook around you and
be distressed,
Look within you and be
depressed,
Look to Jesus and
be at rest.

*T*here is no greater love than the love that holds on where there seems nothing left to hold on to.

Love never fails—never fades out or becomes obsolete or comes to an end.
1 Corinthians 13:8
AMP

Evening, and morning, and at noon, will I pray, and cry aloud: and he shall hear my voice.

Psalm 55:17

*D*aily prayers will diminish your cares.

*B*e like a postage stamp—stick to one thing till you get there.

Be steadfast, immovable, always abounding in the work of the Lord, knowing that your toil is not in vain in the Lord.
1 Corinthians 15:58
NASB

The light in the eyes [of him whose heart is joyful] rejoices the heart of others.

Proverbs 15:30

AMP

A good laugh is sunshine in a house.

*E*ach loving act says loud and clear, "I love you. God loves you. I care. God cares."

Beloved, let us love one another: for love is of God; and every one that loveth is born of God...for God is love.
1 John 4:7,8

*I know whom
I have believed,
and am persuaded
that he is able to
keep that which I
have committed
unto him against
that day.*
2 Timothy 1:12

I have held many things in my hands and lost them all; but the things I have placed in God's hands, those I always possess.

A good deed is never lost; he who sows courtesy reaps friendship, and he who plants kindness gathers love.

Whatsoever a man soweth, that shall he also reap...And let us not be weary in well doing: for in due season we shall reap, if we faint not.
Galatians 6:7,9

She opens her mouth with skillful and godly Wisdom, and in her tongue is the law of kindness— giving counsel and instruction.

Proverbs 31:26

AMP

*K*ind words can be short and easy to speak, but their echoes are truly endless.

*N*othing beats love at first sight except love with insight.

The beginning of wisdom is this: Get wisdom, and whatever else you get, get insight.
Proverbs 4:7
NRSV

29

*Better a meal
of vegetables
where there is love
than a fattened
calf with hatred.
Proverbs 15:17
NIV*

A house is made of
walls and beams; a
home is made of love
and dreams.

*T*he best way to hold a man is in your arms.

The man should give his wife all that is her right as a married woman, and the wife should do the same for her husband.
1 Corinthians 7:3
TLB

A man finds joy in giving an apt reply—and how good is a timely word!
Proverbs 15:23
NIV

Ninety percent of the friction of daily life is caused by the wrong tone of voice.

*F*orgiveness is giving love when there is no reason to....

Blessed are the merciful, For they shall obtain mercy.

Matthew 5:7

NKJV

Thou hast also given me the shield of Thy salvation, And Thy right hand upholds me; And Thy gentleness makes me great.

Psalm 18:35

NASB

Nothing is so strong as gentleness. Nothing is so gentle as real strength.

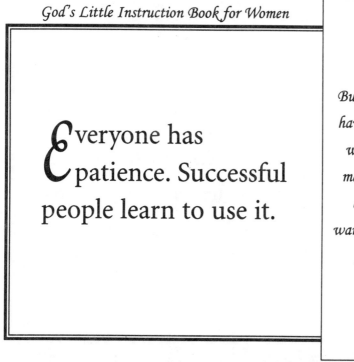

*E*veryone has patience. Successful people learn to use it.

But let patience have her perfect work, that ye may be perfect and entire, wanting nothing.

James 1:4

Keep watching and praying, that you may not come into temptation.

Mark 14:38

NASB

Watch out for temptation— the more you see of it the better it looks.

*I*t is such a comfort to drop the tangles of life into God's hands and leave them there.

Cast your cares on the Lord and he will sustain you.

Psalm 55:22

NIV

A friend loves at all times, and a brother is born for adversity.
Proverbs 17:17
NIV

*F*riendship improves happiness, and abates misery, by doubling our joy, and dividing our grief.

*E*veryone has an invisible sign hanging from his neck saying, "Make me feel important!"

Therefore encourage one another and build each other up, just as in fact you are doing.
1 Thessalonians 5:11
NIV

But encourage one another day after day, as long as it is still called "Today."
Hebrews 3:13
NASB

Y ou cannot do a kindness too soon, because you never know how soon it will be too late!

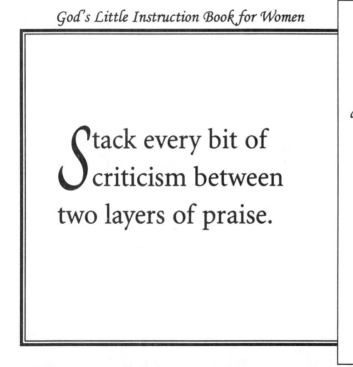

*S*tack every bit of criticism between two layers of praise.

Correct, rebuke and encourage— with great patience and careful instruction.
2 Timothy 4:2
NIV

41

And let us not grow weary in well-doing, for in due season we shall reap, if we do not lose heart.
Galatians 6:9
RSV

*I*n trying times, don't quit trying.

*T*o love what you do and feel that it matters — how could anything be more fun?

When you eat the labor of your hands, You shall be happy, and it shall be well with you.

Psalm 128:2

NKJV

For what is your life? It is even a vapor that appears for a little time and then vanishes away.

James 4:14

NKJV

*L*ife is a coin. You can spend it any way you wish, but you can only spend it once.

*D*iligence is the mother of good fortune.

The hand of the diligent makes one rich.
Proverbs 10:4
NKJV

*A happy heart
makes the face
cheerful, but
heartache crushes
the spirit.*

Proverbs 15:13

NIV

*T*he most wasted of
all days is that on
which one has not
laughed.

You can accomplish more in one hour with God than one lifetime without Him.

Walk in wisdom...
redeeming
the time.
Colossians 4:5

Therefore, take up the full armor of God, that you may be able to resist in the evil day, and having done everything, to stand firm. Stand firm therefore...
Ephesians 6:13,14
NASB

*C*ourage is resistance to fear, mastery of fear. Not the absence of fear.

*T*he art of being wise is the art of knowing what to overlook.

A man's wisdom gives him patience; it is to his glory to overlook an offense. Proverbs 19:11 NIV

49

And let us not be weary in well doing: for in due season we shall reap, if we faint not.
Galatians 6:9

*T*riumph is just "umph" added to try.

*P*eople don't care
how much you
know, until they know
how much you
care...about them.

*And though I
have the gift of
prophecy, and
understand all
mysteries, and all
knowledge; and
though I have all
faith, so that I
could remove
mountains, and
have not charity, I
am nothing.*
1 Corinthians 13:2

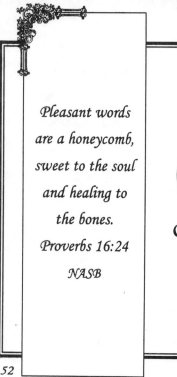

*Pleasant words
are a honeycomb,
sweet to the soul
and healing to
the bones.
Proverbs 16:24
NASB*

*G*ood words are
worth much, and
cost little.

I don't know the secret to success but the key to failure is to try to please everyone.

No one can serve two masters; for either he will hate the one and love the other, or he will hold to one and despise the other.

Matthew 6:24

NASB

53

Bear ye one another's burdens, and so fulfil the law of Christ.

Galatians 6:2

No one is useless in this world who lightens the burden of it to anyone else.

*D*o not follow where the path may lead—go instead where there is no path and leave a trail.

Your ears shall hear a word behind you, saying, "This is the way, walk in it."
Isaiah 30:21
NKJV

If our hearts do not condemn us, we have confidence before God.

1 John 3:21

NIV

*T*here is one thing alone that stands the brunt of life throughout its length; a quiet conscience.

*M*y obligation is to do the right thing. The rest is in God's hands.

If you know that he is righteous, you may be sure that everyone who does right is born of him.

1 John 2:29

RSV

Truly, truly, I say to you, he who believes in Me, the works that I do shall he do also; and greater works than these shall he do; because I go to the Father.

John 14:12

NASB

*E*xpect great things *from* God. Attempt great things *for* God.

*D*ost thou love life?
Then do not
squander time, for that
is the stuff life is
made of.

Remember how
short my time is.
Psalm 89:47

*T*he grass may be greener on the other side, but it still has to be mowed.

Be content with such things as ye have.
Hebrews 13:5

*E*very job is a self-portrait of the person who does it. Autograph your work with excellence.

"Many daughters have done well, But you excel them all."
Proverbs 31:29
NKJV

To be the greatest,
be a servant.
Matthew 23:11
TLB

*T*he greatest achievements are those that benefit others.

*I*f a task is once begun, never leave it till it's done. Be the labor great or small, do it well or not at all.

Whatever your hand finds to do, do it with your might. Ecclesiastes 9:10 NKJV

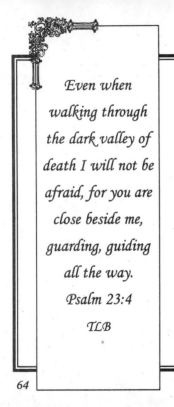

Even when walking through the dark valley of death I will not be afraid, for you are close beside me, guarding, guiding all the way.

Psalm 23:4

TLB

I would rather walk with God in the dark than go alone in the light.

*A*ll our dreams can come true—if we have the courage to pursue them.

Be strong and courageous, and act; do not fear nor be dismayed, for the Lord God, my God, is with you.

1 Chronicles 28:20

NASB

Not forsaking the assembling of ourselves together, as the manner of some is; but exhorting one another: and so much the more, as ye see the day approaching.
Hebrews 10:25

Remember the banana— when it left the bunch, it got skinned.

*D*ecisions can take you out of God's will but never out of His reach.

If we are faithless, he will remain faithful, for he cannot disown himself.
2 Timothy 2:13
NIV

"But let your statement be 'Yes, yes' or 'No, no.'"
Matthew 5:37
NASB

"No" is one of the few words that can never be misunderstood.

*S*ome people complain because God put thorns on roses, while others praise Him for putting roses among thorns.

Finally, brethren, whatsoever things are true, whatsoever things are honest, whatsoever things are just, whatsoever things are pure, whatsoever things are lovely, whatsoever things are of good report; if there be any virtue, and if there be any praise, think on these things.
Philippians 4:8

If it be possible, as much as lieth in you, live peaceably with all men.

Romans 12:18

*T*he bridge you burn now may be the one you later have to cross.

*R*eal friends are those who, when you've made a fool of yourself, don't feel you've done a permanent job.

Love...bears all things, believes all things, hopes all things, endures all things. Love never fails.
1 Corinthians 13:7,8
NKJV

Humble yourselves therefore under the mighty hand of God, that he may exalt you in due time.

1 Peter 5:6

*M*ost people wish to serve God—but only in an advisory capacity.

*C*onscience is God's built-in warning system. Be very happy when it hurts you. Be very worried when it doesn't.

And herein do I exercise myself, to have always a conscience void of offense toward God, and toward men.
Acts 24:16

For ye are bought with a price: therefore glorify God in your body, and in your spirit, which are God's.
1 Corinthians 6:20

*I*f you don't stand for something you'll fall for anything!

*Y*ou should never let adversity get you down—except on your knees.

For I am persuaded, that neither death, nor life, nor angels, nor principalities, nor powers, nor things present, nor things to come...shall be able to separate us from the love of God, which is in Christ Jesus our Lord.

Romans 8:38,39

*It is vain for you
to rise up early,
to sit up late,
to eat the bread
of sorrows: for so
he giveth his
beloved sleep.
Psalm 127:2*

*T*he best bridge
between hope and
despair is often a good
night's sleep.

*I*t is good to remember that the tea kettle, although up to its neck in hot water, continues to sing.

Rejoice evermore. In every thing give thanks: for this is the will of God in Christ Jesus concerning you.
1 Thessalonians 5:16,18

By this shall all men know that ye are my disciples, if ye have love one to another.

John 13:35

*I*t's good to be a Christian and know it, but it's better to be a Christian and show it!

*S*orrow looks back.
Worry looks around.
Faith looks up.

Fixing our eyes on Jesus, the author and perfecter of faith, who for the joy set before Him endured the cross, despising the shame, and has sat down at the right hand of the throne of God.

Hebrews 12:2

NASB

*I will remember
the works of the
Lord: surely I will
remember thy
wonders of old. I
will meditate also
of all thy work,
and talk of thy
doings.
Psalm 77:11,12*

*S*ometimes we are so busy adding up our troubles that we forget to count our blessings.

*G*od can heal a broken heart, but he has to have all the pieces.

My son, give me thine heart.
Proverbs 23:26

But seek first the kingdom of God and His righteousness, and all these things shall be added to you.

Matthew 6:33

NKJV

*B*e more concerned with what God thinks about you than what people think about you.

*T*he best way to get the last word is to apologize.

If you have been trapped by what you said, ensnared by the words of your mouth, then do this, my son, to free yourself, since you have fallen into your neighbor's hands: Go and humble yourself; press your plea with your neighbor!
Proverbs 6:2,3
NIV

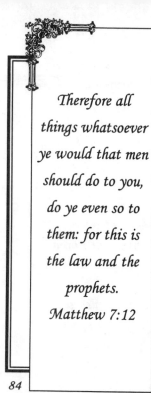

Therefore all things whatsoever ye would that men should do to you, do ye even so to them: for this is the law and the prophets.

Matthew 7:12

*F*orget yourself for others and others will not forget you!

84

*T*he secret of contentment is the realization that life is a gift not a right.

But godliness with contentment is great gain. For we brought nothing into this world, and it is certain we can carry nothing out.
1 Timothy 6:6,7

Be not deceived;
God is not
mocked: for
whatsoever a man
soweth, that shall
he also reap.
Galatians 6:7

*T*hose who bring
sunshine to the lives
of others cannot keep it
from themselves.

*I*t's the little things in life that determine the big things.

Thou hast been faithful over a few things, I will make thee ruler over many things: enter thou into the joy of thy lord.

Matthew 25:21

*Not that I speak
in respect of want:
for I have learned,
in whatsoever
state I am,
therewith to
be content.
Philippians 4:11*

*C*ontentment isn't getting what we want but being satisfied with what we have.

*G*od plus one is always a majority!

If God be for us,
who can be
against us?
Romans 8:31

*A talebearer
revealeth secrets:
but he that is of a
faithful spirit
concealeth the
matter.*

Proverbs 11:13

Whoever gossips *to* you will be a gossip *of* you.

*J*esus is a friend who
knows all your faults
and still loves you
anyway.

*But God
commendeth his
love toward us, in
that, while we
were yet sinners,
Christ died for us.
Romans 5:8*

And be ye kind one to another, tenderhearted, forgiving one another, even as God for Christ's sake hath forgiven you.
Ephesians 4:32

*E*very person should have a special cemetery lot in which to bury the faults of friends and loved ones.

A minute of thought is worth more than an hour of talk.

Set a watch, O Lord, before my mouth; keep the door of my lips.

Psalms 141:3

Let every man be swift to hear, slow to speak, slow to wrath.

James 1:19

Υou can win more friends with your ears than with your mouth.

*I*t's not the outlook but the uplook that counts.

Looking unto Jesus the author and finisher of our faith...
Hebrews 12:2

Starting a quarrel is like breaching a dam; so drop the matter before a dispute breaks out.
Proverbs 17:14
NIV

*I*t isn't hard to make a mountain out of a molehill. Just add a little dirt.

*T*he art of being a good guest is knowing when to leave.

Withdraw thy foot from thy neighbour's house; lest he be weary of thee, and so hate thee.

Proverbs 25:17

These things I have spoken unto you, that in me ye might have peace. In the world ye shall have tribulation: but be of good cheer; I have overcome the world.

John 16:33

*J*esus is a friend who walks in when the world has walked out.

*T*hose who deserve love the least need it the most.

But I say unto you, Love your enemies, bless them that curse you, do good to them that hate you, and pray for them which despitefully use you, and persecute you. Matthew 5:44

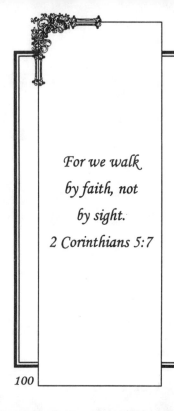

*For we walk
by faith, not
by sight.*

2 Corinthians 5:7

$\mathcal{F}$aith is daring the soul to go beyond what the eyes can see.

A critical spirit is like poison ivy—it only takes a little contact to spread its poison.

But avoid worldly and empty chatter, for it will lead to further ungodliness.

2 Timothy 2:16

NASB

Let no corrupt communication proceed out of your mouth, but that which is good to the use of edifying, that it may minister grace unto the hearers.
Ephesians 4:29

*T*wo things are hard on the heart— running up stairs and running down people.

*H*umor is to life what shock absorbers are to automobiles.

Then our mouth was filled with laughter, And our tongue with singing. Then they said among the nations, "The Lord has done great things for them."

Psalm 126:2

NKJV

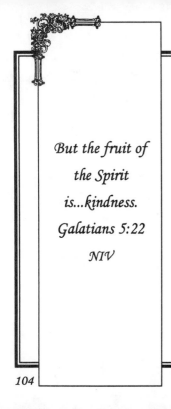

*But the fruit of
the Spirit
is...kindness.
Galatians 5:22
NIV*

Kindness is the oil
that takes the
friction out of life.

*O*ur days are identical suitcases— all the same size—but some people can pack more into them than others.

Be very careful, then, how you live—not as unwise but as wise, making the most of every opportunity.
Ephesians 5:15,16
NIV

For if ye forgive men their trespasses, your heavenly Father will also forgive you: But if ye forgive not men their trespasses, neither will your Father forgive your trespasses.

Matthew 6:14,15

To forgive is to set a prisoner free and discover the prisoner was YOU.

*T*he heart is the happiest when it beats for others.

Greater love hath no man than this, that a man lay down his life for his friends.

John 15:13

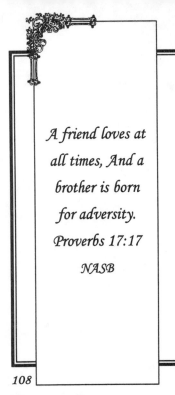

A friend loves at all times, And a brother is born for adversity.

Proverbs 17:17

NASB

A true friend never gets in your way unless you happen to be going down.

*L*aughter is the brush that sweeps away the cobwebs of the heart.

A happy heart is a good medicine and a cheerful mind works healing, but a broken spirit dries the bones.

Proverbs 17:22

AMP

109

And Jesus looking upon them saith, With men it is impossible, but not with God: for with God all things are possible.

Mark 10:27

*G*od has a history of using the insignificant to accomplish the impossible.

*P*eople may doubt what you say, but they will always believe what you do.

...for the tree is known and recognized and judged by its fruit.
Matthew 12:33
AMP

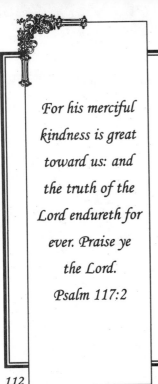

For his merciful kindness is great toward us: and the truth of the Lord endureth for ever. Praise ye the Lord.

Psalm 117:2

Kindness is a language which the deaf can hear and the blind can see.

I make it a rule of Christian duty never to go to a place where there is not room for my Master as well as myself.

Don't be teamed with those who do not love the Lord...How can a Christian be a partner with one who doesn't believe?
2 Corinthians 6:14,15
TLB

Do all things without murmurings and disputings.
Philippians 2:14

*J*esus can turn water into wine, but He can't turn your whining into anything.

*T*he smallest deed is better than the greatest intention!

Let us not love [merely] in theory or in speech but in deed and in truth—in practice and in sincerity.
1 John 3:18
AMP

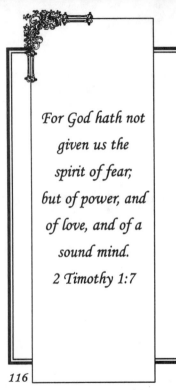

For God hath not given us the spirit of fear, but of power, and of love, and of a sound mind.

2 Timothy 1:7

I've suffered a great many catastrophes in my life. Most of them never happened.

*G*uilt is concerned with the past. Worry is concerned about the future. Contentment enjoys the present.

Not that I am implying that I was in any personal want, for I have learned how to be content (satsified to the point where I am not disturbed or disquieted) in whatever state I am.
Philippians 4:11
AMP

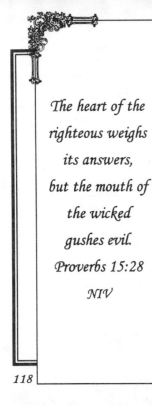

The heart of the righteous weighs its answers, but the mouth of the wicked gushes evil.

Proverbs 15:28

NIV

$\mathcal{P}$eople with tact have less to retract.

*B*eing at peace with yourself is a direct result of finding peace with God.

And the peace of God, which passeth all understanding, shall keep your hearts and minds through Christ Jesus.
Philippians 4:7

How long are ye slack to go to possess the land, which the Lord God of your fathers hath given you?

Joshua 18:3

*I*f you want to make an easy job seem mighty hard, just keep putting off doing it.

*L*ove sees through a telescope not a microscope.

Love endures long and is patient and kind...it takes no account of the evil done to it— pays no attention to a suffered wrong.
1 Corinthians 13:4,5
AMP

This is the day the Lord has made; let us rejoice and be glad in it.

Psalm 118:24

NIV

*L*ife is not a problem to be solved, but a gift to be enjoyed.

A pint of example is worth a barrel full of advice.

Brethren, join in following my example, and observe those who walk according to the pattern you have in us.

Philippians 3:17

NASB

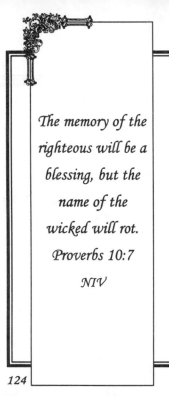

The memory of the righteous will be a blessing, but the name of the wicked will rot.

Proverbs 10:7

NIV

*B*eware lest your footprints on the sand of time leave only the marks of a heel.

*I*f you were given a nickname descriptive of your character, would you be proud of it?

A good name is rather to be chosen than great riches.
Proverbs 22:1

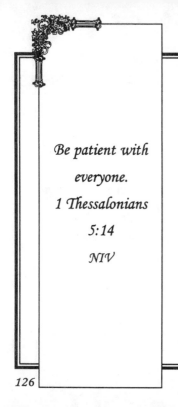

Be patient with everyone.
1 Thessalonians
5:14
NIV

*I*t's easy to identify people who can't count to ten. They're in front of you in the supermarket express lane.

*T*act is the art of making a point without making an enemy.

Reckless words pierce like a sword, but the tongue of the wise brings healing.
Proverbs 12:18
NIV

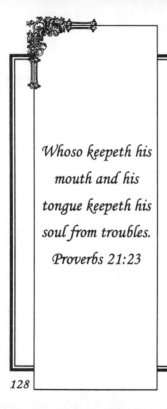

Whoso keepeth his mouth and his tongue keepeth his soul from troubles.

Proverbs 21:23

*S*ilence is one of the hardest arguments to refute.

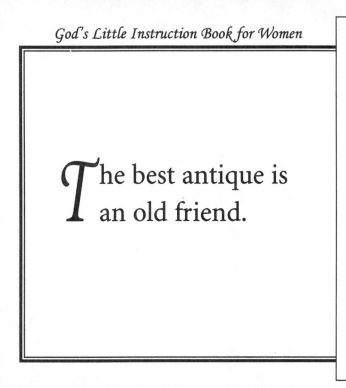

*T*he best antique is
an old friend.

*Your own friend
and your father's
friend, forsake
not...Better is a
neighbor who is
near [in spirit]
than a brother
who is far off
[in heart].*
Proverbs 27:10
AMP

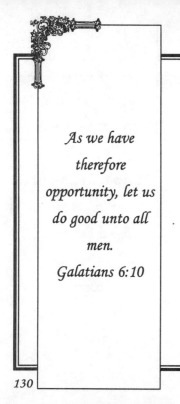

As we have therefore opportunity, let us do good unto all men.

Galatians 6:10

*I*f you can't feed a hundred people then just feed one.

*T*he trouble with stretching the truth is that it's apt to snap back.

A false witness shall not be unpunished, and he that speaketh lies shall not escape.

Proverbs 19:5

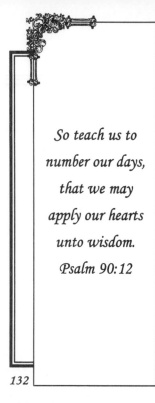

So teach us to number our days, that we may apply our hearts unto wisdom.
Psalm 90:12

Birthdays are good for you. Statistics show that the people who have the most live the longest.

*F*aults are thick
where love is thin.

*And above all
things have
fervent charity
among yourselves:
for charity shall
cover the
multitude of sins.
1 Peter 4:8*

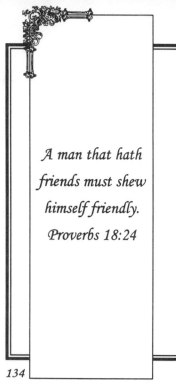

A man that hath friends must shew himself friendly.

Proverbs 18:24

*T*he only way to have a friend is to be one.

*T*he world wants your best but God wants your all.

Thou shalt love the Lord thy God with all thy heart, and with all thy soul, and with all thy mind.

Matthew 22:37

*Do not forsake
wisdom, and she
will protect
you....When you
walk, your steps
will not be
hampered; when
you run, you will
not stumble.
Proverbs 4:6,12
NIV*

*H*indsight explains
the injury that
foresight would have
prevented.

*D*o not in the darkness of night, what you'd shun in broad daylight.

The night is far spent, the day is at hand: let us therefore cast off the works of darkness, and let us put on the armour of light.

Romans 13:12

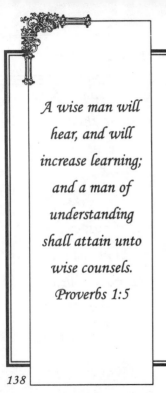

A wise man will hear, and will increase learning; and a man of understanding shall attain unto wise counsels.

Proverbs 1:5

I am defeated, and know it, if I meet any human being from whom I find myself unable to learn anything.

*H*onesty is the first chapter of the book of wisdom.

Provide things honest in the sight of all men.

Romans 12:17

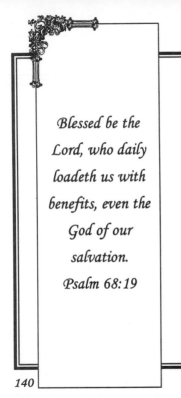

Blessed be the Lord, who daily loadeth us with benefits, even the God of our salvation.

Psalm 68:19

*G*od always gives His best to those who leave the choice with Him.

A lot of people mistake a short memory for a clear conscience.

And herein do I exercise myself, to have always a conscience void of offense toward God, and toward men.

Acts 24:16

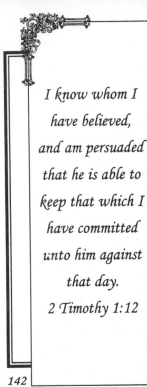

I know whom I have believed, and am persuaded that he is able to keep that which I have committed unto him against that day.

2 Timothy 1:12

*F*aith is not belief without proof, but trust without reservation.

A day hemmed in prayer is less likely to unravel.

Pray about everything; tell God your needs, and don't forget to thank him for his answers. If you do this, you will experience God's peace...His peace will keep your thoughts and your hearts quiet and at rest.
Philippians 4:6,7
TLB

Now flee from youthful lusts, and pursue righteousness, faith, love and peace, with those who call on the Lord from a pure heart.

2 Timothy 2:22

NASB

When you flee temptations don't leave a forwarding address.

A coincidence is a small miracle where God prefers to remain anonymous.

Who can put into words and tell the mighty deeds of the Lord? Or can show forth all the praise [that is due Him]?

Psalm 106:2

AMP

And the peace of God, which transcends all understanding, will guard your hearts and your minds in Christ Jesus.
Philippians 4:7
NIV

*S*ometimes the Lord calms the storm; sometimes He lets the storm rage and calms His child.

*T*he past should be a springboard not a hammock.

This one thing I do, forgetting those things which are behind, and reaching forth unto those things which are before.

Philippians 3:13

Bless the Lord, O my soul...who crowneth thee with lovingkindness and tender mercies; Who satisfieth thy mouth with good things.
Psalm 103:1,4,5

The teacher asked the pupils to tell the meaning of lovingkindness. A little boy jumped up and said, "Well, if I was hungry and someone gave me a piece of bread that would be kindness. But if they put a little jelly on it, that would be loving kindness."

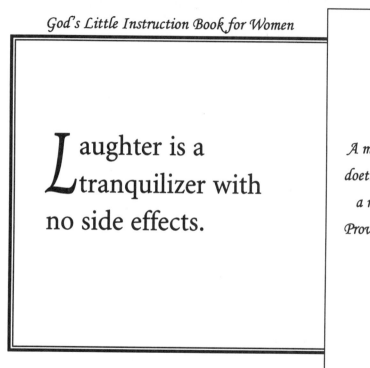

*L*aughter is a tranquilizer with no side effects.

A merry heart doeth good like a medicine.
Proverbs 17:22

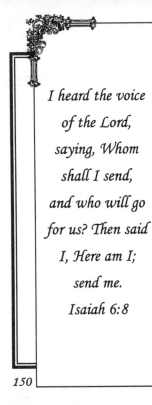

I heard the voice of the Lord, saying, Whom shall I send, and who will go for us? Then said I, Here am I; send me.

Isaiah 6:8

God never asks about our ability or our inability—just our availability.

*W*hether you think
you can or think
you can't, you're right.

As he thinketh in
his heart,
so is he.
Proverbs 23:7

Give, and it shall be given unto you.
Luke 6:38

The best way to cheer yourself up is to cheer up somebody else.

*F*ailure isn't falling
down. It's staying
down.

*A just man falleth
seven times, and
riseth up again.
Proverbs 24:16*

I am fearfully and wonderfully made.
Psalm 139:14

Nobody can make you feel inferior without your consent.

References

Acknowledgements

Ruth Bell Graham (8), Mother Teresa (9,28,130), Jean Hodges (10), George M. Adams (12), Glen Wheeler (13), Helen Pearson (15), Joseph Addison (16), Cyrus (17), Henry Ward Beecher (18), G.W.C. Thomas (21), Betty Mills (22), Josh Billings (23,128), Thackeray (24), Joyce Heinrich and Annette La Placa (25), Joyce Earline Steelburg (26), St. Basil (27), Catherine Graham (43), Lillian Dickson (44), Cervantes (45), Sebastian-Roche (46), Mark Twain (48,112,116), William James (49), Zig Ziglar (51), William Feather (52), Bill Cosby (53), Charles Dickens (54), Euripedes (56), Martin Luther King, Jr. (57), William Carey (58), Benjamin Franklin (59), Dennis Waitley (62), Mary Gardner Brainard (64), Walt Disney (65), Arnold H. Glasgow (108), Mort Walker (109), Richard Exley (110), John Newton (113), Mark Steele (114), Olin Miller (119), Joseph P. Dooley (122), June Henderson (126), Dr. John Olson (127), Reverend

Larry Lorenzoni (132), James Howell (133), Ralph Waldo Emerson (134), Charles H. Spurgeon (137), George Herbert Palmer (138), Thomas Jefferson (139), Jim Elliot (140), Doug Larsen (141), Elton Trueblood (142), Ivern Ball (147), Merceline Cox (149), Henry Ford (151), Mary Pickford (153), Eleanor Roosevelt (154).

Dear Reader:

If you would like to share with us a couple of your favorite quotes or ideas on the subject of being a successful woman we'd love to hear from you. Our address is:

Honor Books
P.O. Box 55388, Dept. J.
Tulsa, Oklahoma 74155

Additional Copies of this book and other titles
in the *God's Little Instruction Book* series
are available at your local bookstore.

God's Little Instruction Book
God's Little Instruction Book II
God's Little Instruction Book for Mom
God's Little Instruction Book for Dad
God's Little Instruction Book for Graduates
God's Little Instruction Book for Students
God's Little Instruction Book for Kids
God's Little Instruction Book for Couples
God's Little Instruction Book for Men
God's Little Instruction Book – Special Gift Edition
God's Little Instruction Book Daily Calendar

Honor Books
P.O. Box 55388
Tulsa, Oklahoma 74155